AFGHANISTAN

By Sophie Washburne
and Joanne Mattern

EXPLORING
WORLD
CULTURES

Cavendish Square

Published in 2024 by Cavendish Square Publishing, LLC
2544 Clinton Street, Buffalo, NY 14224

Second Edition

Website: cavendishsq.com

Library of Congress Cataloging-in-Publication Data

Names: Washburne, Sophie, author. | Mattern, Joanne, 1963- author.
Title: Afghanistan / Sophie Washburne and Joanne Mattern.
Description: Second edition. | Buffalo, NY : Cavendish Square Publishing, 2024. | Series: Exploring world cultures | Includes index.
Identifiers: LCCN 2023026572 | ISBN 9781502669902 (library binding) | ISBN 9781502669896 (paperback) | ISBN 9781502669919 (ebook)
Subjects: LCSH: Afghanistan--Juvenile literature. | Afghanistan--Civilization.
Classification: LCC DS351.5 .M38 2024 | DDC 958.1--dc23/eng/20230614
LC record available at https://lccn.loc.gov/2023026572

Writers: Joanne Mattern; Sophie Washburne (second edition)
Editor: Jennifer Lombardo
Copyeditor: Danielle Haynes
Designer: Andrea Davison-Bartolotta

The photographs in this book are used by permission and through the courtesy of: Cover FatCamera/iStockphoto.com; p. 4 tunasalmon/Shutterstock.com; p. 5 Dennis W Donohue/Shutterstock.com; p. 6 Germanova Antonina/Shutterstock.com; p. 7 Robert J. Martin/Shutterstock.com; p. 8 Dimitrios Karamitros/Shutterstock.com; pp. 9, 10 Salma Bashir Motiwala/Shutterstock.com; p. 11 Leonid Altman/Shutterstock.com; p. 12 Evgeny Freyer/Shutterstock.com; p. 13 Peter Loud/Shutterstock.com; p. 15 (bottom) Lauren Suryanata/Shutterstock.com; p. 15 (top) NOWAK LUKASZ/Shutterstock.com; pp. 16, 20, 21, 27 timsimages.uk/Shutterstock.com; p. 17 Piero_Facci/Shutterstock.com; p. 18 matteo bedendo/Shutterstock.com; p. 19 Trent Inness/Shutterstock.com; p. 22 xshlabs/Shutterstock.com; p. 23 FotograFFF/Shutterstock.com; p. 24 PJF Military Collection/Alamy Stock Photo; p. 25 Wandering views/Shutterstock.com; p. 26 solmaz daryani/Shutterstock.com; p. 28 FarzoTastyFood/Shutterstock.com; p. 29 warishasrat73/Shutterstock.com.

CPSIA compliance information: Batch #CW24CSQ: For further information contact Cavendish Square Publishing LLC at 1-877-980-4450.

Printed in the United States of America

CONTENTS

INTRODUCTION

The 12th-largest country in Asia is called Afghanistan. Its full name is the Islamic **Emirate** of Afghanistan. It's landlocked, or surrounded by land on all sides.

Afghanistan is a beautiful country, with high mountains, rocky deserts, and flowing rivers. The weather in much of the country is very hot and dry.

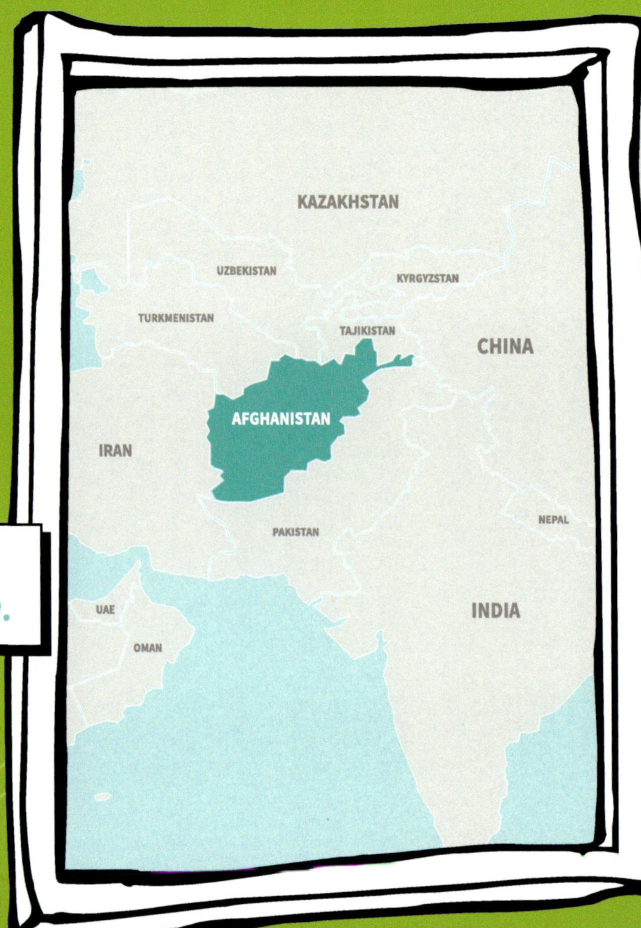

This map shows Afghanistan's location.

About 40 million people live in Afghanistan. The country's population includes several different **ethnic** groups. About 40 different languages are spoken in Afghanistan! The two most common languages are Dari and Pashto. Most people in Afghanistan live in the countryside, but there are also several large cities.

The Afghan people have had to deal with a lot of problems in their country's history. Some of these problems are still going on today. This makes many parts of the country dangerous, or unsafe, for travelers as well as for Afghans.

Snow leopards live in Afghanistan's mountains, where the weather is colder.

GEOGRAPHY

Afghanistan is bordered by six countries. They are Iran, Turkmenistan, Uzbekistan, Tajikistan, China, and Pakistan. Afghanistan covers 251,827 square miles (652,230 square kilometers).

The Hindu Kush mountains are in the northeast and central parts of the country. The Baba Mountains are also in the central part of Afghanistan. The Paropamisus Mountains are in the west. Most Afghans live in the valleys between mountains. These areas are more fertile, or better for growing crops.

The Hindu Kush mountains have some very high peaks, or tops.

FACT! Afghanistan's capital and largest city is Kabul.

This picture shows the Helmand River.

The nation's most important rivers are the Helmand, Kabul, and Hari. Much of the southern part of the country is covered by rocky deserts. The largest is called the Registan.

CITY OR COUNTRY?

Life is very different in Afghan cities than in the countryside. The cities are crowded with people and **traffic**. In the country, there are many open spaces where people can farm food and animals.

HISTORY

People have lived in Afghanistan for more than 50,000 years. Over time, many people have led the country. In 1219 CE, Genghis Khan took over the country. After his death, Afghanistan broke into smaller states. A chief ruled each state.

During the 19th century, Great Britain and Russia fought over Afghanistan. The country finally became independent in 1919. A king and queen led Afghanistan until 1973, when it became a **republic**.

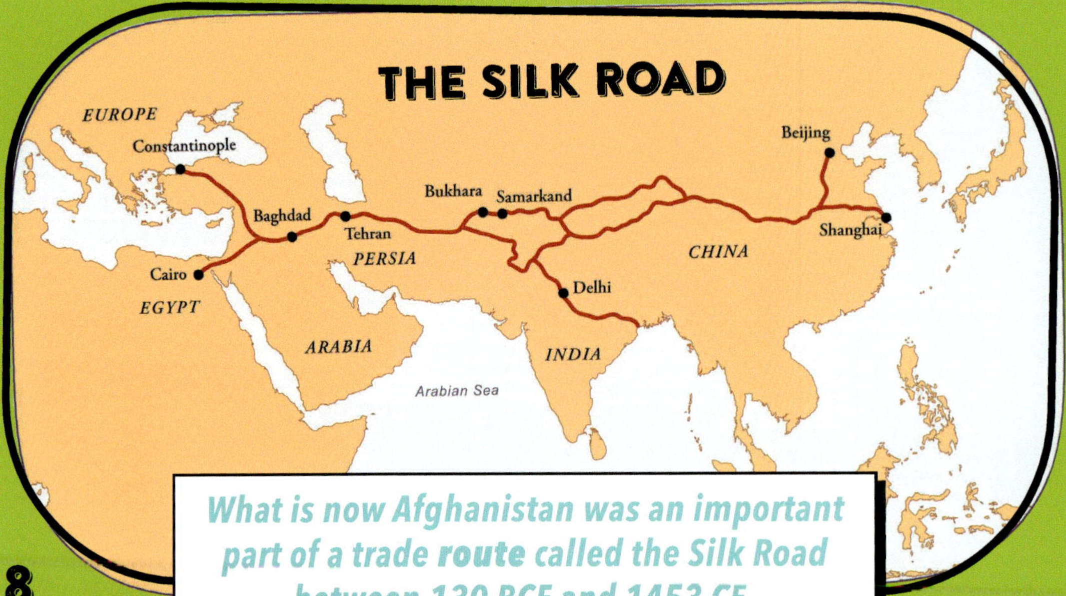

What is now Afghanistan was an important part of a trade **route** called the Silk Road between 130 BCE and 1453 CE.

In 1996, a group called the Taliban took over Kabul and then had power over most of Afghanistan. The Taliban had a lot of rules, especially for women. In 2001, the United States and Great Britain went to war with the Taliban.

FACT!

Darius the Great made Afghanistan part of the Persian **Empire**. It was part of this empire from 522 BCE to 330 BCE.

Taliban members (shown here) have hurt many of their own people.

THE PEOPLE'S GOVERNMENT

From 2004 to 2021, Afghanistan had a government much like that of the United States. There were three parts, or branches, of government that worked together to keep the country running well.

GOVERNMENT

In 2021, the U.S. Army left Afghanistan. Right away, the Taliban took over again. They made new laws based on Islamic law. Most girls aren't allowed to go to school, and women aren't allowed to have jobs.

Hibatullah Akhundzada is the leader of the country as of 2023. He appointed everyone else in the government.

FACT!

The ***punishments*** for breaking the law in Afghanistan can be very scary.

Afghan voters elected Hamid Karzai as Afghanistan's first president in 2004.

The Afghan government has a 30-person Leadership Council that helps Akhundzada run the country, but he has all the power. There's also a **cabinet** made up of 33 people called ministers. The Cabinet of Afghanistan makes sure people follow the laws.

NOT LISTENING

In 2004, the Afghan people worked together to write a new **constitution**. When the Taliban took over again, they threw out the constitution and made new laws without asking the people what they wanted.

When the Taliban took over, they got rid of Afghanistan's flag (left) and replaced it with their own (right).

THE ECONOMY

Many Afghans take care of themselves by growing their own food and raising animals for meat and fur. Afghanistan sells rugs and dried fruit to other countries.

For years, the poppy has been a big part of Afghanistan's **economy**. People use this flower to make illegal drugs such as opium and heroin. The Taliban started destroying poppy fields when they took over.

Afghan farmers have lost a lot of money because the Taliban destroyed their poppy fields without giving them something else to grow.

SANCTIONS

Sanctions are economic punishments that are given when a country does something other countries don't like. Many countries sanctioned Afghanistan in 2021 because they disagreed with the Taliban's actions.

Overall, Afghanistan's economy is not doing well. While other armies were in the country, their governments were giving a lot of money to Afghanistan—about 40 percent of all the money in the Afghan economy. When these armies left and those payments stopped, the Afghan economy was badly hurt.

FACT!

When COVID-19 was spreading quickly around the world, many countries—including Afghanistan—had economic problems.

Handmade rugs are a big part of the Afghan economy.

THE ENVIRONMENT

Afghanistan has about 3,000 different species, or kinds, of plants. Many of these can be used to make medicine. There are many kinds of flowers aside from poppies, such as tulips and lilies. Afghan farmers grow foods such as wheat, rice, grapes, and onions.

Wild sheep and goats live high in the mountains. Snow leopards, brown bears, and wolves live in the thick forests. Herds of gazelle and oryx live on the plains. Brown trout and other fish swim in the country's rivers.

One problem facing animals as well as people in Afghanistan is deforestation. This is when too many trees are cut down. Deforestation can destroy animals' homes and cause floods that wash away crops.

FACT!

Like the rest of the world, Afghanistan is facing problems caused by ***climate change.***

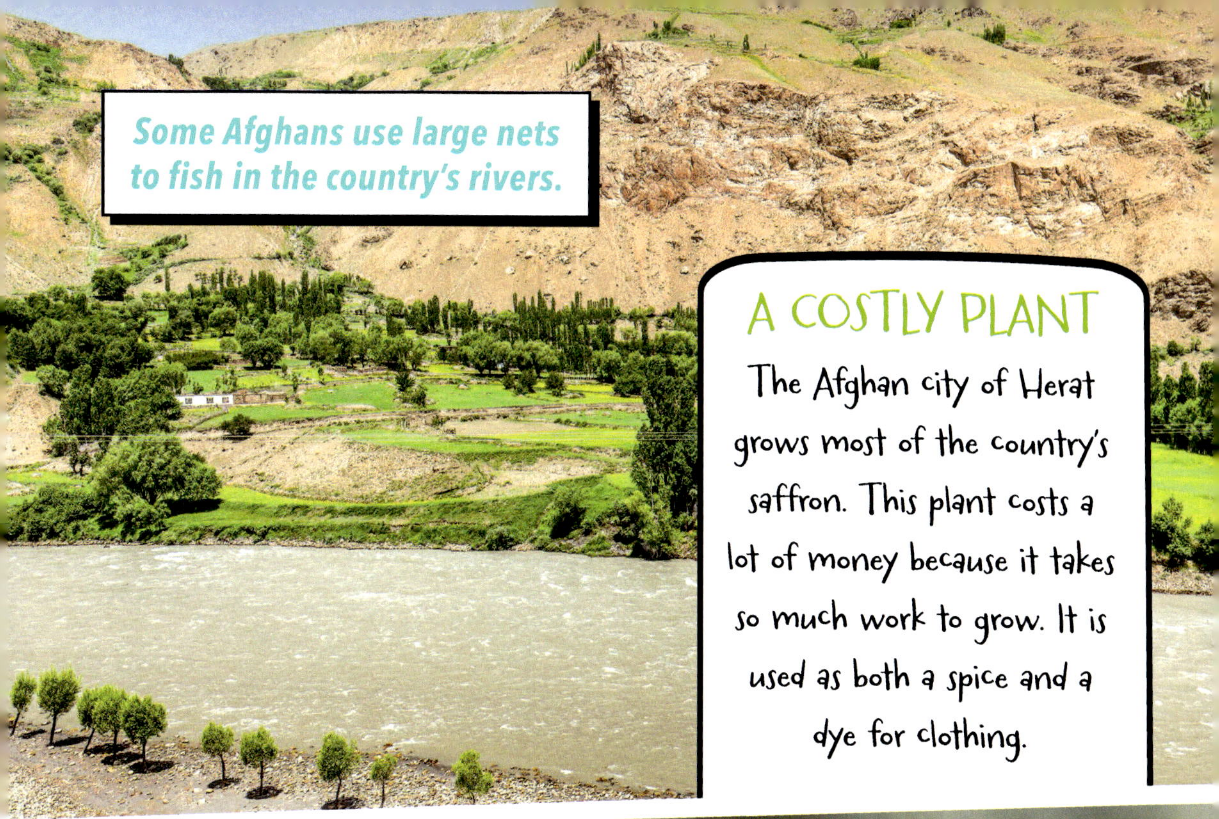

Some Afghans use large nets to fish in the country's rivers.

A COSTLY PLANT

The Afghan city of Herat grows most of the country's saffron. This plant costs a lot of money because it takes so much work to grow. It is used as both a spice and a dye for clothing.

A small animal called the jerboa stays alive in the desert by getting its water from the food it eats.

THE PEOPLE TODAY

The largest group living in Afghanistan today are the Pashtuns. They speak a language called Pashto. Most live between the Hindu Kush mountains and the Indus River.

FACT!

The Pashtuns make up about 42 percent of Afghans, and the Tajiks make up about 27 percent.

This Pashtun man is making bread by hand.

ETHNIC SPLITS

There are two sects, or groups, of Muslims, called Sunni and Shia. Most Pashtuns, Tajiks, and Uzbeks are Sunni. Hazaras are the largest group of Shia.

Tajiks are the second-largest group. They came to Afghanistan from Iran many years ago. Most Tajiks live in the eastern mountains and are shepherds and farmers. The third-largest ethnic group is the Hazaras. They live mostly in central Afghanistan. Other ethnic groups include Uzbeks, Aimaks, Balochs, and Turkmen.

Afghanistan's many ethnic groups give the country a lot of different ways of life. However, nearly all of them share a religion: Islam.

Some of the Afghan ethnic groups have taken the Hazaras' land, stolen their belongings, and practiced **genocide** against them.

LIFESTYLE

Family is the most important part of life for Afghans. People do what's best for the whole family, not just for themselves. Family honor is very important, so people try not to do things that will make their family look bad.

Families often live together in one house or group of houses. Men are in charge of business and make most of the rules. Women are in charge of the housework and children.

In the Afghan countryside, many people live in a type of house called a yurt.

For years, it has been hard for many Afghans to lead a normal life because of all the fighting that's been happening in the country. As of 2021, 2.3 million Afghan people have become refugees.

FACT!

After an Afghan couple gets married, they usually move in with the husband's family.

An Afghan girl stands in a refugee camp.

REFUGEE CAMPS

A refugee is a person who has to leave their home to get away from danger. Many Afghan refugees go to Iran and Pakistan, where they live in camps. Many never return to their homes.

RELIGION

In Afghanistan, 99.7 percent of the people are Muslim. The rest include Jews, Sikhs, Hindus, and Christians. Most non-Muslims have had to leave the country so they aren't hurt or killed by the Taliban.

Muslims follow the teachings of the Prophet Muhammad. These are written in a holy book called the Quran.

The Taliban say women have to be covered from head to toe. Islam gives women a choice about this, but the Taliban took that choice away.

Muslims pray five times a day by kneeling on prayer rugs and bowing their heads to the floor. They have to face the Muslim holy city of Mecca when they do this. They can pray at home or in a place called a mosque.

MANY DON'T AGREE

The Taliban made Afghanistan's laws based on Muslim laws. However, most Muslims around the world don't agree with the way the Taliban leaders force people to act. They believe Islam is a religion, or belief system, that can be peaceful—not hurtful.

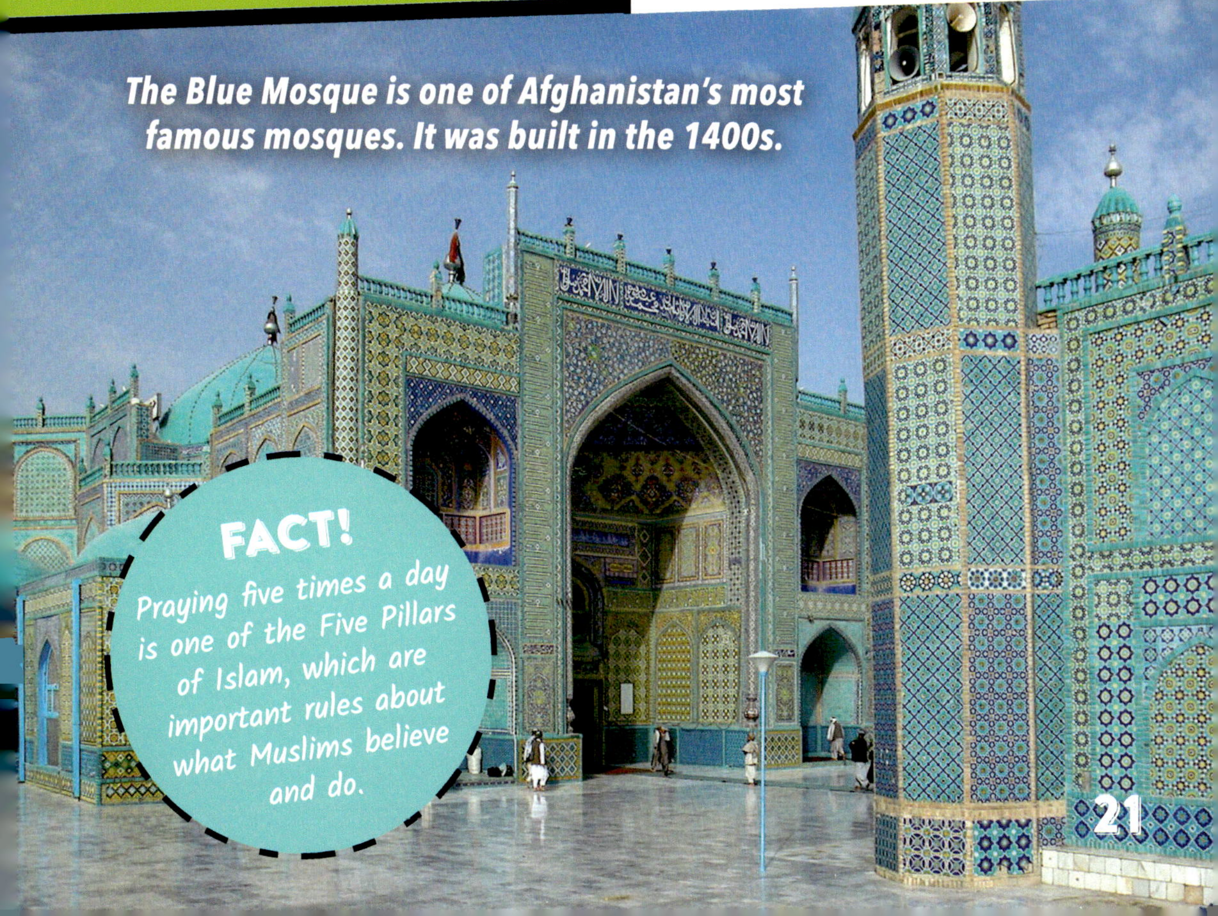

The Blue Mosque is one of Afghanistan's most famous mosques. It was built in the 1400s.

FACT!

Praying five times a day is one of the Five Pillars of Islam, which are important rules about what Muslims believe and do.

LANGUAGE

The two official languages of Afghanistan are Pashto and Dari. The Pashtuns speak Pashto. Other ethnic groups, including the Tajiks and Hazaras, speak Dari. Both are written in Arabic script, or writing.

FACT!
Some people learned to speak English, French, Russian, or other languages if they went to school before the Taliban took over.

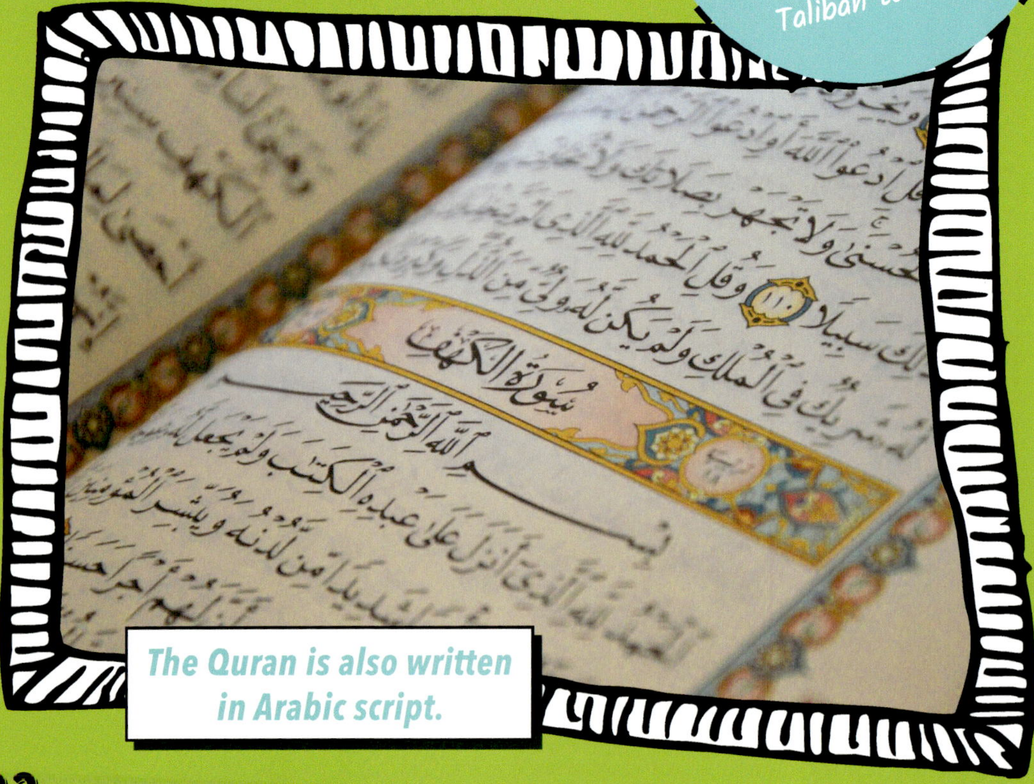

The Quran is also written in Arabic script.

Children learn both Pashto and Dari in school. Afghans use Dari in business. Many people speak two or more languages. In addition to Pashto and Dari, they might speak Uzbek, Turkoman, Baluchi, or another language. Today, girls are only allowed to go to school until sixth grade, so many will have trouble speaking and writing correctly in later years.

ARABIC WRITING

Arabic is a spoken language as well as a written one. There are many different kinds, or dialects, of spoken Arabic. However, nearly all written Arabic is the same, so everyone who knows Arabic can read it even if they don't speak a certain dialect.

An official language is one a country uses for government business, such as money and passports.

ARTS AND FESTIVALS

Art has a long history in Afghanistan. The country is known for its colorful wool carpets, or rugs. These carpets are made by hand and include many different colors and patterns. Each ethnic group or area has its own special patterns. However, since 2021, people don't have much time or money to make art for fun. Carpets are still made because they sell well.

FACT!

When the Taliban ruled the country from 1996 to 2001, all music and dancing were banned.

This picture shows Afghans dancing at a talent show at a U.S. Army base in 2008.

The *attan* is the national dance of Afghanistan. Men stand in a circle and move their feet quickly as they clap their hands.

Holidays are mostly Muslim holy days. One exception is the Afghan New Year (Nowruz), or Afghanistan Day, on March 21.

A SAD DAY

In 2001, the Taliban blew up two big **statues** of the Buddha (the main figure in Buddhism) from the 6th century. People around the world begged them not to do it because of how special this art was, but they did not listen.

Afghans who have left their country use Afghanistan Day to call for an end to the Taliban's rule and to remember the old ways that are being destroyed.

FUN AND PLAY

Life in Afghanistan has been hard for a long time, but in the past, Afghans often still had a chance to have fun. Dancing and playing music were popular ways to spend time. Afghan men also gathered at teahouses to drink tea and share news with one another.

FACT!
The first time the Taliban were in power, they banned all sports. The second time, they banned only women's sports.

This picture from 2019 shows boys and girls at an Afghan school.

Since 2021, however, 94 percent of Afghans say things in the country have gotten too bad to enjoy life. Many adults are out of work. The Taliban don't allow most girls to go to school. Women aren't allowed to leave the house without a good reason. Boys can go to school, but many have to work instead to help their families.

PLAYING BUZKASHI

Afghans have played the sport of buzkashi for about 800 years. Players ride on horses and fight to grab the "ball," which is the body of an animal—often a goat. To score a point, a player must carry the body from one end of the playing field to the other and back again.

The Taliban have arranged buzkashi games.

FOOD

Rice and wheat are two important parts of Afghan meals. Afghans prepare rice in many ways. They serve it plain or with meat. They also season it with different spices. Pilau is a popular mix of rice, meat, vegetables, and spices.

A SWEET TREAT

Jalebi is a popular dessert in Afghanistan and other countries. It's made by mixing flour with yogurt. This mixture is fried in oil and then covered in a syrup made with rose water, saffron, or honey.

This picture shows an Afghan dish of fried eggplant with yogurt sauce.

Many fruits, vegetables, and nuts grow in Afghanistan. These foods are a big part of the diet. Afghans also eat cheese, eggs, chicken, and lamb.

Naan is a common flatbread. Afghans use naan to scoop up foods such as *borani kadoo*. They make this dish with pumpkin, spices, and tomatoes, with garlic yogurt on the side.

FACT!

Since 2021, food has become hard to find and pay for in Afghanistan. An average meal may be only a piece of naan.

Afghans often sit around a large cloth or carpet on the floor to enjoy their meal.

GLOSSARY

cabinet: A group of advisers to the leader of a country.

climate change: Long-lasting changes to Earth's weather patterns caused by human activity.

constitution: A document that lays out the beliefs and laws of a country.

economy: The way goods and services are made and sold.

emirate: A country that is ruled by a Muslim leader called an emir.

empire: A group of political areas under one leader.

ethnic: Related to people who have a common national or cultural tradition.

genocide: The deliberate destruction of a racial, political, or cultural group.

passport: A document governments give their citizens to allow them to travel to other countries.

punishment: A penalty for doing something that is seen as bad or wrong.

republic: A state where power is held by the people and their elected representatives.

route: A course of travel.

statue: A piece of art made out of something solid, such as rock.

traffic: A crowded mass of vehicles.

FIND OUT MORE

Books

Brundle, Harriet. *Islam*. Norfolk, UK: BookLife, 2023.

Havelka, Jacqueline. *Afghanistan*. Hollywood, FL: Mason Crest, 2023.

Peterson, Christy. *Welcome to Afghanistan with Sesame Street*. Minneapolis, MN: Lerner Publications, 2022.

Websites

Britannica Kids: Afghanistan
kids.britannica.com/kids/article/Afghanistan/345822
Read about the geography, people, and history of Afghanistan.

National Geographic Kids: Afghanistan
kids.nationalgeographic.com/geography/countries/article/afghanistan
Learn more about Afghanistan, including how the Taliban took over in 2021.

Video

YouTube: "Day in the Life of a Child in Afghanistan"
www.youtube.com/watch?v=VsyYaNrhAIY
See what it's like to be a kid in Afghanistan.

Publisher's note to educators and parents: Our editors have carefully reviewed these websites to ensure that they are suitable for students. Many websites change frequently, however, and we cannot guarantee that a site's future contents will continue to meet our high standards of quality and educational value. Be advised that students should be closely supervised whenever they access the internet.

INDEX